THERE'S MORE...
MUCH MORE

GULLIVER BOOKS

HARCOURT BRACE & COMPANY

SAN DIEGO   NEW YORK   LONDON

THERE'S MORE...
MUCH MORE

Written by

SUE ALEXANDER

Illustrated by

PATIENCE BREWSTER

Library of Congress Cataloging-in-Publication Data
Alexander, Sue, 1933-
There's more, much more.
"Gulliver books."
Summary: Squirrel and Sherri celebrate spring by
collecting it in their May baskets.
[1. Spring—Fiction] 1. Brewster, Patience, ill.
II. Title.
PZ7.A3784Th 1987   [E]   86-33632
ISBN 0-15-200605-2

B C D E

Printed in Hong Kong

The illustrations/paintings in this book were done in pencil and watercolor on
    Aquabee satin finish and Strathmore kid finish bristol paper.
This book was printed on 120 GSM Matte.
The text type was set in Minister Light by Central Graphics, San Diego,
    California.
The display type was set in Announcement Italic by Thompson Type, San Diego,
    California.
Printed and bound by South China Printing Company, Hong Kong
Designed by Dalia Hartman
Production supervision by Warren Wallerstein and Rebecca Miller

From the beginning…
For Jane Yolen

—S. A.

Thank you to the Fairy Sisters:
Grammie Withie for daffodil hill and a world of love,
and Daudear for her heart full of perpetual spring and
her head topped with its bounty.

—P. B.

Squirrel walked by with a basket on his arm.

"Where are you going, Squirrel?" asked Sherri.

"To fill my May basket," said Squirrel.

"What's that?" Sherri asked.

"Well," said Squirrel, "it's a basket filled with spring."

"With spring?" asked Sherri. "How do you fill a basket with spring?"

"Get a basket, and I'll show you," said Squirrel.

Sherri found a basket. She took her hair-ribbon and made a handle.

Then she went with Squirrel.

"That's spring," said Squirrel. And he pointed to two blue flower buds nestled on a tiny stem.

"Is that all of spring?" asked Sherri as she put the stem in her basket.

"No, there's more . . . much more. Come along," said Squirrel.

"That's spring," said Squirrel. And he pointed to a green leaf slowly unfolding on a tree.

"Is that all of spring?" asked Sherri as she put the leaf carefully in her basket.

"No, there's more . . . much more," said Squirrel. "Come along."

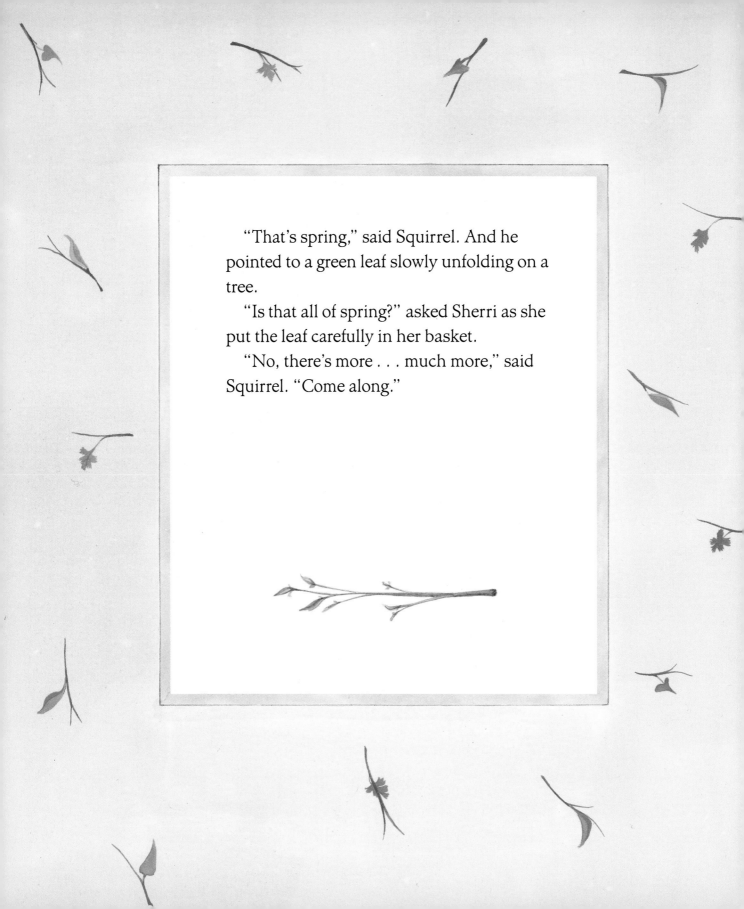

And farther into the forest they went.

"That's spring," said Squirrel. And he pointed to a twig with a butterfly cocoon clinging to its side.

Sherri put the twig with the cocoon in her basket.

"Is that all of spring?" she asked.

"No, there's more . . . much more," said Squirrel.

Squirrel showed Sherri the wild straw-berries beginning to blossom.

He showed her the new sap that ran from the trees.

He showed her baby earthworms coming out of their eggs in the ground.

One by one Sherri put them in her basket.

Then she asked, "Is that all of spring?"

"No, there's more . . . much more," said Squirrel.

"But my basket is full," said Sherri. And she sat down on a rock under a tree.

"Some of spring won't fit in your basket," said Squirrel. "Not even if your basket were as big as the forest."

Sherri looked around. She didn't see anything that big.

"What do you mean?" she asked.

Squirrel smiled.

"Close your eyes," he said. "And take a deep breath."

Sherri closed her eyes and breathed deeply.

"What did you smell?" asked Squirrel.

Sherri thought for a minute.

"Sweet flowers, dew on the grass, and fresh earth," she answered.

"That's spring, too," said Squirrel. "And smells won't fit in your basket."

"Oh," said Sherri. "Is that all of spring?"

"No, there's more . . . much more," said Squirrel. "Open your ears and be very still."

Sherri sat very still.

"Now listen!" said Squirrel.

Sherri listened.

"What did you hear?" asked Squirrel.

"Lots of things," Sherri said. "I heard the stream rushing over the rocks. I heard the birds calling to each other as they built their nests. I heard the wind whispering through the leaves on the trees."

"That's spring, too," said Squirrel. "And sounds won't fit in your basket."

"No, they won't," Sherri agreed. Then she said, "Is that all of spring?"

Squirrel shook his head.

"No," he said, "there's still more . . . much more. Tell me how you feel."

"How I feel?" asked Sherri.

"How you feel right *now*," said Squirrel.
Sherri thought.

Then she said, "I feel happy—and sad.
I feel like jumping—and tiptoeing. I feel like
shouting—and sighing. I feel all *mixed-up!*"

"That's spring, too," said Squirrel. "And
feelings won't fit in your basket either."

"Oh!" said Sherri. "I feel something else, too. I feel awake—and sleepy."

Squirrel laughed. "That's spring, too," he said.

Sherri yawned.

"In fact, Squirrel," she said, "I'm so sleepy that I'm going to take a nap now."

And she lay down on the new grass.

Just as her eyes were closing Sherri said, "Thank you, Squirrel, for showing me spring."

"You're welcome," whispered Squirrel.

And then he went to fill his own May basket.